THE BEST OF

Chocolate

THE BEST OF

Chocolate

A COOKBOOK

Mary Goodbody & Brooke Dojny

Food Photography by Ellen Silverman

CollinsPublishersSanFrancisco

A Division of HarperCollins*Publishers*

First published in USA 1994 by CollinsPublishersSanFrancisco
1160 Battery Street, San Francisco, CA 94111

Produced by Smallwood and Stewart, Inc.,
New York City

© 1994 Smallwood and Stewart, Inc.

Editor: Kathy Kingsley
Food Styling: Deborah Mintcheff
Prop Styling: Betty Alfenito

Photography credits: Robert Opie: p. 1, 14. Mathias Oppersdorff: p. 7.
Hershey's Community Archives: p. 44. Boys Syndication/ Michael Boys: 84.

Library of Congress Cataloguing-in-Publication Data

Goodbody, Mary.
    The best of chocolate : a cookbook / Mary Goodbody and
Brooke Dojny : food photography by Ellen Silverman
p. cm.
Includes index
ISBN 0-00-255254-X
1. Cookery (Chocolate) I. Dojny, Brooke. II. Title.
TX767.C5G657 1993
641.6'374--dc20   93-34472
                                                    CIP

Printed in China

Contents

Introduction

In these pages is a collection of seductive, rich, and, at times, unapologetically decadent recipes using chocolate. We understand that for many, a day without chocolate is incomplete; for others, a chocolate dessert is an occasional indulgence to be anticipated excitedly and savored slowly. This book is intended for chocolate lovers of all kinds. Each recipe captures chocolate at its very best, whether in a rich cake or tart or in the lightest soufflé. Together they serve as a celebration of this most sybaritic and well-loved food. After all, chocolate stands in a class by itself and as such deserves unabashed admiration.

When the Spanish explorer Cortez first tasted the bitter drink called *chocolatl* offered him by the Aztec emperor Montezuma, he knew he had stumbled onto something extraordinary. After he introduced chocolate to the Spanish court, clever culinarians added sugar, thus initiating a love affair between Europeans and chocolate that still flourishes. By the end of the nineteenth century, American cooks, borrowing from their European

Women drying cocoa beans, Grenada

cousins, began using chocolate to flavor cakes and cookies. Then an American named Milton Hershey came up with the idea of mass-producing milk chocolate bars, and the American mania for chocolate began in earnest.

Chocolate begins with cocoa beans that are fermented, roasted, shelled, and crushed into nibs (meat). The nibs, which contain about 53 percent cocoa butter, are ground and processed into a solid mass called chocolate liquor. When allowed to solidify, chocolate liquor becomes unsweetened or bitter chocolate. To produce semisweet, bittersweet, or milk chocolate, the chocolate liquor is further refined by adding varying amounts of cocoa butter and other ingredients such as sugar, vanilla, milk solids, and lecithin. White chocolate is the only variety of chocolate that does not contain chocolate liquor. Cocoa powder is produced by removing most of the cocoa butter from the liquor and grinding and sifting the resulting mass.

All of these chocolates have their baking and cooking uses, although milk and white chocolate are less frequently found in recipes because their high percentage of milk proteins can make heating problematic. Among chocolate aficionados, the rule about which chocolate to use for cooking is similar to the one applied to wine: Don't cook with a chocolate you wouldn't eat. (The sole exception is unsweetened chocolate.) But there is no doubt that the richer the chocolate, the deeper and more complex the flavor of the finished product. The chocolates used in our recipes are readily available in supermarkets across the country.

Putting this collection together was a joyful, delicious experience because we were working with chocolate in all its glory day after day. We trust that with the help of these recipes, chocolate will be part of your daily ~ or at least weekly ~ life, too.

Mary Goodbody & Brooke Dojny

Best-Ever Chocolate Chip Cookies

*Whether you use regular-size or mini chocolate chips,
these cookies will be immediately recognizable as just about the
best incarnation imaginable of the all-American favorite.
Mini chips make the cookies a little more chocolaty, while the
regular-size chips remain more defined when baked.*

½ cup (1 stick) unsalted butter, softened

¾ cup packed light brown sugar

¼ cup granulated sugar

1 large egg

1 teaspoon pure vanilla extract

1¼ cups all-purpose flour

½ teaspoon baking soda

¼ teaspoon salt

6 ounces (1 cup) semisweet chocolate chips, or 9 ounces (1½ cups) semisweet mini chips

¾ cup coarsely chopped pecans or walnuts (optional)

Preheat the oven to 375°F. Lightly grease 2 baking sheets. In a large bowl, using an electric mixer set at high, cream together the butter and both sugars until smooth and fluffy. Add the egg and vanilla and beat until smooth.

In a small bowl, whisk together the flour, baking soda, and salt. Reduce the mixer speed to medium and beat in the flour mixture until just blended. Stir in the chocolate chips, and the nuts if desired.

Drop about 1½ tablespoonfuls of dough onto the baking sheets, spacing them about 2 inches apart. Bake for 9 to 11 minutes, or until browned around the edges. Set the baking sheets on wire racks to cool for 5 minutes, then transfer the cookies to the racks to cool completely. Store in an airtight container for up to 3 days. **Makes about 1½ dozen cookies.**

English chocolate advertisement from the 1920s.

Double-Chocolate Cracks

These big, dark, chewy cookies are not for the timid.
Made with two kinds of chocolate, they are great with a glass
of cold milk or a mug of hot coffee.

1 ¼ cups packed dark
   brown sugar

½ cup (1 stick) unsalted butter

3 ounces unsweetened chocolate, coarsely chopped

1 teaspoon instant espresso
   or instant coffee powder

1 large egg

2 teaspoons pure vanilla
   extract

1 ¼ cups all-purpose flour

¾ teaspoon baking soda

¼ teaspoon salt

12 ounces (2 cups) semisweet
   chocolate chips

In a heavy medium-size saucepan, combine the brown sugar, butter, chocolate, and espresso. Cook over low heat, stirring frequently, until the chocolate is melted. The mixture will look grainy. Transfer to a medium bowl and cool until lukewarm, stirring occasionally. Whisk the egg and vanilla into the cooled chocolate mixture.

In a small bowl, whisk together the flour, baking soda, and salt. Add the flour mixture to the chocolate and stir until blended. Stir in the chocolate chips, and nuts if desired. Chill the dough for 30 minutes, or until firm enough to shape into cookies.

Preheat the oven to 350°F. Lightly grease 2 baking sheets.

Drop heaping tablespoonfuls of dough onto the baking sheets, spacing them about 1 ½ inches apart. Dampen your fingers in cold water and shape each cookie into neat, slightly flattened rounds.

Bake for 10 to 13 minutes, or until the tops are cracked and the edges are set. The centers will be slightly soft. Set

the baking sheets on wire racks to cool for 5 minutes. Transfer the cookies to the racks to cool completely. Store in an air-tight container for up to 2 days. **Makes about 30 cookies.**

English chocolate advertisement from the 1920s.

14

Dark and White Chocolate Chunk Cookies

Picture p. 2

*These might be considered home-style
chocolate chip cookies all dressed up for a night on the town.*

½ cup (1 stick) unsalted butter, softened

½ cup granulated sugar

½ cup packed light brown sugar

1 large egg

1¼ teaspoons pure vanilla extract

1¼ cups all-purpose flour

½ teaspoon baking soda

¼ teaspoon salt

6 ounces bittersweet chocolate, chopped into ¼-inch pieces

4 ounces white chocolate, chopped into ¼-inch pieces

½ cup chopped walnuts (optional)

Preheat the oven to 350°F. Lightly grease 2 baking sheets.

In a large bowl, using an electric mixer set at high, cream together the butter and both sugars until smooth and fluffy. Add the egg and vanilla and beat until smooth.

In a small bowl, whisk together the flour, baking soda, and salt. With the mixer set at medium, beat in the flour mixture until just blended. Stir in both kinds of chocolate chunks, and the nuts if desired.

Drop about 1½ tablespoonfuls of dough onto the baking sheets, spacing them about 2 inches apart. Bake for 11 to 13 minutes, or until browned around the edges. Set the baking sheets on wire racks to cool for 5 minutes, then transfer the cookies to the racks to cool completely. Store in an airtight container for up to 3 days. **Makes about 1½ dozen cookies.**

Chocolate Shortbread

*Classic shortbread, with its characteristic buttery,
melt-in-the-mouth texture, is made even more divine by the addition
of cocoa powder. Dutch-processed (alkalized) cocoa powder
is recommended because it is slightly less bitter, but nonalkalized
cocoa will also produce nice results.*

1 cup plus 2 tablespoons all-purpose flour

½ cup plus 2 tablespoons unsweetened Dutch-processed cocoa powder

⅛ teaspoon salt

¾ cup (1½ sticks) unsalted butter, softened

⅔ cup confectioners' sugar

1 teaspoon pure vanilla extract

In a small bowl, whisk together 1 cup of the flour, ½ cup of the cocoa powder, and the salt.

In a large bowl, using an electric mixer set at high, cream together the butter and sugar until light and fluffy. Add the vanilla and beat until smooth. Reduce the mixer speed to low and beat in the flour mixture until just combined.

Gather the dough into a ball and flatten into a 7- or 8-inch disk. Wrap in plastic and refrigerate for at least 1 hour, or freeze for at least 20 minutes, until firm.

Preheat the oven to 350°F. Sprinkle a work surface with the remaining 2 tablespoons of flour and cocoa. Divide the dough in half. Chill one half while working with the other. Roll the dough out to a ½-inch thickness. Cut it into 2-inch squares, or use 2-inch cookie cutters to cut out shapes. Put the cookies on ungreased baking sheets, spacing them about 1 inch apart. Prick each cookie several times with a fork. Gather the scraps and roll them out to make more cookies. Repeat with the remaining dough, using more flour and cocoa if necessary.

Bake for 15 to 17 minutes, or until the shortbread is firm to the touch. The cookies should not darken. Set the baking sheets on wire racks to cool for 5 minutes, then transfer the cookies to the racks to cool completely. Store in an airtight container for up to 5 days. **Makes about 2 dozen cookies.**

NOTE: To prepare the shortbread dough in the food processor, use the metal blade to process the butter, sugar, and vanilla until smooth. Add the flour-cocoa mixture and process by pulsing on and off until the dough begins to form a ball. Proceed with the recipe as directed.

Macadamia–Milk Chocolate Chip Cookies

Studded with creamy milk chocolate chips and rich, buttery macadamia nuts, these simple cookies are a luscious departure from more familiar chocolate chip cookies. Because the nuts are lightly salted, there is no need to add salt to the dough.

2¼ cups all-purpose flour

1 teaspoon baking soda

1 cup (2 sticks) unsalted butter, softened

¾ cup packed dark brown sugar

¾ cup granulated sugar

2 large eggs

1½ teaspoons pure vanilla extract

12 ounces (2 cups) milk chocolate chips

1 cup chopped macadamia nuts

Preheat the oven to 350°F. Lightly grease 2 baking sheets. In a small bowl, whisk together the flour and baking soda.

In a large bowl, using an electric mixer set at high, cream together the butter and both sugars until smooth and fluffy. Reduce the mixer speed to medium and beat in the eggs and vanilla until smooth. Beat in the flour mixture until just blended. Stir in the chocolate chips and nuts.

Drop about 1½ tablespoonfuls of dough onto the baking sheets, spacing them about 2 inches apart. Bake for 9 to 11 minutes, or until browned around the edges and puffy in the center. Set the baking sheets on wire racks to cool for 5 minutes, then transfer the cookies to the racks to cool completely. Store in an airtight container for up to 3 days. **Makes 4 to 5 dozen cookies.**

Chunky Peanut Butter–Chocolate Chip Bars

These homespun bar cookies are perfect for the cookie jar, and because they are good travelers they are always welcome in lunch boxes and care-packages.

1 1/3 cups all-purpose flour
1 teaspoon baking powder
1/4 teaspoon baking soda
1/4 teaspoon salt
2/3 cup extra-chunky
    peanut butter

1/4 cup (1/2 stick) unsalted
    butter, softened
1 cup packed light brown sugar
2 large eggs
1 teaspoon pure vanilla extract
8 ounces (1 1/3 cups) semisweet
    chocolate chips

Preheat the oven to 350°F. Grease a 9-inch square baking pan. In a small bowl, whisk together the flour, baking powder, baking soda, and salt.

In a medium bowl, using an electric mixer set at high, cream together the peanut butter, butter, and brown sugar until fluffy. Add the eggs and vanilla and beat until well blended. Reduce the mixer speed to low and beat in the flour mixture until just combined. Stir in the chocolate chips.

Scrape the batter into the prepared pan and spread it evenly. Bake in the center of the oven for 30 to 35 minutes, or until the surface is golden brown and a toothpick inserted into the center comes out clean. Set the pan on a wire rack to cool completely. When cool, cut into 16 large or 24 medium bars. Store in an airtight container for up to 3 days. **Makes 16 to 24 bars.**

Rich Walnut Fudge Brownies

For brownies that are chewy and fudgy in the the middle rather than cakelike, bake for about 30 minutes, or until a few crumbs cling to a toothpick inserted into the center.

3 ounces unsweetened
   chocolate, coarsely chopped
½ cup (1 stick) unsalted butter
¼ cup packed light brown sugar
1 cup granulated sugar

⅔ cup all-purpose flour
½ teaspoon baking powder
2 large eggs
1 teaspoon pure vanilla extract
1½ cups chopped walnuts

Preheat the oven to 350°F. Grease and flour an 8-inch square baking pan. Tap out the excess flour.

Melt the chocolate with the butter and both sugars in the top of a double boiler set over barely simmering (not boiling) water, stirring until smooth. Or microwave the mixture in a microwave-safe container, uncovered, on medium (50 percent) power for 2 to 4 minutes, stirring once, until the chocolate is shiny; remove from the microwave and stir until smooth and melted. Transfer to a large bowl and cool to lukewarm.

In a small bowl, whisk together the flour and baking powder. Set aside.

Add the eggs and vanilla to the cooled chocolate mixture and stir until blended. Stir in the flour mixture until just combined. Stir in the walnuts.

Scrape the batter into the prepared pan and spread evenly. Bake for 35 to 40 minutes, or until a toothpick inserted into the center comes out clean. Set the pan on a wire rack to cool completely. When cool, cut the brownies into 16 squares. Store in an airtight container for up to 3 days. **Makes 16 bars.**

the sugar, salt, and vanilla until blended. Stir in the cooled chocolate mixture. Add the flour and nuts and stir until blended.

Scrape the batter into the prepared pan and spread evenly. Bake in the center of the oven for 30 to 35 minutes, or until a skewer or toothpick inserted into the center comes out clean. Set the pan on a wire rack to cool completely.

Prepare the ganache: In a small saucepan, heat the cream over medium heat until small bubbles appear around the edges. Remove the pan from the heat, add the chocolate, and stir until melted and smooth. If necessary, set the pan over very low heat to help melt the chocolate.

Pour the cream mixture into a medium bowl set over a larger bowl filled with ice cubes and water. Stir the ganache for 5 minutes, or until cold to the touch. Remove the bowl from the ice bath. Using an electric mixer set at high, beat the ganache for 1 minute, or until thickened to a spreadable consistency.

Spread the ganache over the cooled squares. Chill for at least 1 hour, then cut into 25 squares. Store in an airtight container in the refrigerator for up to 3 days. **Makes 25 small squares.**

Chocolate-Raspberry Linzer Bars

*Austrians long ago discovered the delectable
combination of a short, cinnamon-kissed crust filled with raspberry
jam and almonds, a creation called linzertorte. When cocoa is added to
the crust and bittersweet chocolate spread over it, the traditional
takes on new ~ and delicious ~ dimensions.*

⅔ cup blanched sliced almonds

⅔ cup sugar

⅔ cup all-purpose flour

2 tablespoons unsweetened
   nonalkalized cocoa powder

¼ teaspoon cinnamon

⅛ teaspoon salt

¼ cup (½ stick) unsalted butter,
   chilled & cut into small pieces

1 large egg

1 teaspoon pure vanilla extract

½ teaspoon grated lemon zest

1½ ounces unsweetened
   chocolate, coarsely chopped

¼ cup seedless raspberry
   preserves, preferably
   all-fruit or sugar-free

Preheat the oven to 325°F. Grease a 9-inch square baking pan.

In a food processor fitted with the metal blade, combine half the almonds and half the sugar. Process until the nuts are finely chopped but not ground. Add the remaining sugar, the flour, cocoa, cinnamon, and salt and process until blended.

Add the butter and process just until the mixture resembles coarse meal. Add the egg, vanilla, and lemon zest, and process by pulsing on and off until the dough gathers together.

Scrape the dough into the prepared pan and press it into an even layer. Bake in the center of the oven for 20 to 22 minutes, or until set.

Meanwhile, melt the chocolate in the top of a double boiler set over barely

simmering (not boiling) water, stirring until smooth. Or microwave the chocolate in a microwave-safe container, uncovered, on medium (50 percent) power for 2 to 4 minutes, stirring once, until the chocolate is shiny; remove from the microwave and stir until smooth and melted.

Remove the crust from the oven. (Leave the oven on.) Brush with the melted chocolate, then chill for 10 min-

utes, or until the chocolate is set.

Chop the remaining almonds. Spread the raspberry preserves over the chocolate and sprinkle with the almonds. Bake for 22 to 25 minutes longer, or until the preserves are bubbling and the almonds are a light golden color.

Set the pan on a wire rack to cool completely. When cool, cut into 24 large or 36 small bars. Store in an airtight container for up to 3 days. **Makes 24 to 36 bars.**

Rich Chocolate-Almond Cake with Dark Chocolate Glaze

For fans of rich, moist chocolate cake, this almost flourless single-layer confection will be an instant winner. Sheathed in a shiny dark glaze, it is pure elegance.

Chocolate-Almond Cake:

3 ounces bittersweet chocolate, coarsely chopped

1 ounce unsweetened chocolate, coarsely chopped

2 teaspoons instant espresso or instant coffee powder

2 tablespoons brandy

1 teaspoon pure vanilla extract

1 cup blanched slivered almonds

⅓ cup all-purpose flour

½ cup (1 stick) unsalted butter, softened

⅔ cup sugar

¼ teaspoon salt

3 large eggs

Dark Chocolate Glaze:

½ cup heavy cream

4 ounces bittersweet chocolate, coarsely chopped

¼ cup sliced almonds, for decoration (optional)

Prepare the cake: Preheat the oven to 350°F. Grease an 8- or 9- inch round cake pan. Line the bottom with parchment or waxed paper.

Melt both chocolates in the top of a double boiler set over barely simmering (not boiling) water, stirring until smooth.

Or microwave the chocolates in a microwave-safe container, uncovered, on medium (50 percent) power for 2 to 4 minutes, stirring once, until the chocolate is shiny; remove from the microwave and stir until smooth and melted. Stir in the espresso until dissolved. Add the

brandy and vanilla; stir until blended. Set aside to cool to lukewarm.

In a food processor fitted with the metal blade, combine the almonds and flour and process until the nuts are finely ground but not oily. Set aside.

In a medium bowl, using an electric mixer set at high, cream together the butter, sugar, and salt until light and fluffy. Add the eggs one at a time, beating well after each addition. Reduce the mixer speed to low and beat in the cooled chocolate mixture. Add the almond mixture and beat until just combined.

Scrape the batter into the prepared pan and bake in the center of the oven for 20 to 35 minutes, or until a skewer or toothpick inserted halfway between the edge and the center comes out clean. The center should be moist and pudding-like. If using a 9-inch pan, test the cake after 20 minutes; if using an 8-inch pan, test it after 25 minutes. During baking, the cake may puff up in the center and crack; it will fall during cooling.

Set the pan on a wire rack to cool for 20 minutes. Then invert it onto the rack, remove the pan and peel off the paper, and let it cool completely.

Prepare the glaze: In a small saucepan, heat the cream over medium heat until small bubbles appear around the edges. Remove the pan from the heat, add the chocolate, and stir until smooth and glossy. Cool to room temperature.

Set the cake, on the wire rack, over a baking sheet lined with waxed paper. Spoon the glaze over the cake and smooth it over the top and sides with a large metal spatula. Transfer to a serving plate and chill for about 2 hours, or until the glaze is set. Decorate the top of the cake with the sliced almonds, if desired, and allow it to come to room temperature before cutting into thin slices. **Serves 8 to 10.**

Black and White Cupcakes

*Cupcakes are easy, portable, and always festive. After
you frost these dark chocolate cakes with the fluffy white buttercream,
decorate them according to whim or the season. For example, use
rainbow sprinkles for birthday parties, gumdrops for Christmas, candy
corn for Halloween, and jelly beans for Easter. Or serve them with
no more adornment than the snowy white frosting.*

Cupcakes:

3 ounces unsweetened
   chocolate, coarsely chopped

2 cups all-purpose flour

2 teaspoons baking soda

½ teaspoon salt

½ cup (1 stick) unsalted butter,
   softened

1¼ cups granulated sugar

1 cup packed light brown sugar

3 large eggs

1 teaspoon pure vanilla extract

1 cup sour cream

1 cup boiling water

Buttercream Frosting:

¼ cup (½ stick) unsalted
   butter, softened

3 tablespoons solid
   vegetable shortening

3 cups confectioners' sugar

2 teaspoons pure vanilla extract

¼ cup heavy cream or milk

Colored sprinkles, candy corn,
   gumdrops, or jelly beans, for
   decoration (optional)

Prepare the cupcakes: Preheat the oven to 350°F. Grease 24 muffin-pan cups or line them with paper liners.

Melt the chocolate in the top of a double boiler set over barely simmering (not boiling) water, stirring until smooth. Or microwave the chocolate in a microwave-safe container, uncovered, on medium (50 percent) power for 2 to 4 minutes, stirring once, until the

chocolate is shiny; remove from the microwave and stir until smooth and melted. Set aside to cool to lukewarm.

In a small bowl, whisk together the flour, baking soda, and salt.

In a large bowl, using an electric mixer set at high, cream the butter until light and fluffy. Add both sugars and beat until well blended. Add the eggs one at a time, beating well after each addition. Add the vanilla and beat for 2 minutes. Reduce the mixer speed to low and beat in the cooled melted chocolate and the sour cream. Beat in the flour mixture until just blended. Add the boiling water and beat until just smooth.

Spoon the batter into the prepared cups, filling them about three quarters full. Bake for 22 to 25 minutes, or until springy to the touch and a skewer or toothpick inserted into the center comes out clean. Set the pans on wire racks to cool completely.

Prepare the Frosting: In a large bowl, using an electric mixer set at high, cream together the butter and shortening until light and fluffy. Reduce the mixer speed to medium and gradually beat in the confectioners' sugar. Beat in the vanilla. Add the cream and beat until smooth, light, and fluffy. Spread the frosting over the top of the cupcakes and decorate with candy, if desired. **Makes 24 cupcakes.**

NOTE: The cupcake batter can also be used to make two 8- or 9-inch cake layers. Bake them for 30 to 35 minutes.

Chocolate Angel Food Cake

Cocoa and grated semisweet chocolate combine to enhance the delicate flavor of this light and airy cake. Be sure to avoid any traces of yolk in the egg whites, which would prevent them from whipping to their fullest. For the best flavor and texture, serve the cake on the day it's made, by itself or with fresh fruit.

¾ cup sifted cake flour

¼ cup unsweetened Dutch-processed cocoa powder

1½ cups granulated sugar

3 ounces semisweet chocolate, grated

12 large egg whites, at room temperature

1 teaspoon cream of tartar

¼ teaspoon salt

1½ teaspoons pure vanilla extract

1 teaspoon lemon juice

Confectioners' sugar, for dusting (optional)

Preheat the oven to 325°F. Have ready an ungreased 9½-inch angel food or tube pan. If the pan does not have a removable bottom, line the bottom with parchment or waxed paper.

Sift together the flour, cocoa, and half the sugar. Remove 3 tablespoons of the flour mixture and toss it with the grated chocolate. Set both mixtures aside.

In a large bowl, using an electric mixer set at low, beat the egg whites until foamy. Add the cream of tartar and salt, increase the mixer speed to medium, and beat until soft peaks form. Gradually add the remaining sugar and beat until the whites are shiny and stiff peaks form. Add the vanilla and lemon juice and beat until just blended.

Sift the flour mixture 3 tablespoons at a time over the egg whites; using a rubber spatula, gently and thoroughly fold the flour into the whites. Then fold in the choco-

late mixture until no white streaks remain.

Gently scrape the batter into the pan. Smooth the top and gently tap the pan on the countertop to remove any air bubbles. Bake in the lower third of the oven for 50 to 60 minutes, or until the cake is golden brown and the top springs back when pressed lightly.

If the cake pan has metal "feet," invert it onto them. If not, invert the pan over the neck of a bottle to prevent the cake from falling during cooling. Allow the cake to cool completely in the pan, 2 to 3 hours.

To unmold, run a thin, sharp knife around the outside edge and the central cone of the pan, and lift it off. Then cut between the removable bottom and the cake, or peel off the parchment paper. Transfer the cake to a serving plate and lightly dust with confectioners' sugar, if desired. Slice with a serrated knife. **Serves 10 to 12.**

Fabulous Flourless Mocha Mousse Cake

*This is, without a doubt, one of the most seductive desserts.
The mousse cake is light as a feather but has a deep, rich, intense chocolate
flavor you won't be able to resist, particularly if it's topped with
whipped cream and raspberries. The cake tastes best on the day it's made,
although you can refrigerate it overnight before serving. For even
greater chocolate intensity, use all bittersweet chocolate rather than
a combination of semisweet and unsweetened.*

9 ounces semisweet chocolate, coarsely chopped

1 ounce unsweetened chocolate, coarsely chopped

½ cup (1 stick) unsalted butter, softened

2 tablespoons dark rum

2 teaspoons instant espresso powder

½ cup heavy cream, chilled

2 tablespoons confectioners' sugar

4 large eggs

3 tablespoons granulated sugar

Whipped cream, for decoration (optional)

½ pint fresh raspberries, for decoration (optional)

4 to 6 ounces semisweet, bittersweet, milk, or white chocolate, for chocolate curls (optional)

Preheat the oven to 350°F. Grease an 8- or 9-inch square baking pan and line the bottom with parchment or waxed paper.

Melt both chocolates with the butter, rum, and espresso in the top of a double boiler set over barely simmering (not boiling) water, stirring until smooth.

Or microwave the mixture in a microwave-safe container, covered loosely with waxed paper, on medium (50 percent) power for 2 to 4 minutes, stirring once, until the chocolate is shiny; remove from the microwave and stir until smooth and melted. Set aside to cool to lukewarm.

In a chilled medium bowl, using an electric mixer set at high, beat the cream with the confectioners' sugar until soft peaks form. Chill until ready to use.

In a large stainless steel bowl, combine the eggs and granulated sugar. Set the bowl over simmering water and whisk for about 2 minutes, or until the sugar dissolves and the mixture is warm to the touch. Remove the bowl from the water and, using an electric mixer set at medium speed, beat the egg mixture with clean, dry beaters for 4 to 5 minutes, or until very pale yellow and tripled in volume.

Whisk the chocolate briefly until smooth and glossy. Stir the chocolate into the beaten eggs until well blended. Using a rubber spatula, gently and thoroughly fold in the whipped cream until no white streaks remain.

Scrape the batter into the prepared pan. Set the pan in a larger pan and add enough hot water to the large pan to come halfway up the sides of the cake pan. Bake in the water bath for 25 to 33 minutes, or until the cake is set on the top and a skewer or toothpick inserted into the center comes out just slightly moist.

Remove both pans from the oven and set them on a wire rack. Let the cake cool in the water bath for about 30 minutes. Remove the cake pan from the water. Using a knife, loosen the sides of the cake, and invert it onto a serving plate. Peel off the paper.

To make the curls: Melt the chocolate and spread thinly on a marble slab or on the back of a baking sheet. If using marble, let the chocolate cool until firm; if using a baking sheet, chill for 5 to 10 minutes, or until firm but not brittle. Using a metal spatula held at a 45° angle, scrape the chocolate from the surface to form curls. To prevent melting, handle curls with a wooden skewer and chill until ready to use.

Cut the cake into squares and serve warm or at room temperature, with whipped cream, raspberries, and chocolate curls, if desired. **Serves 8 to 10.**

Chocolate Pecan Loaf Cake

This is one of those cakes you will make time and time again. It's easy to prepare and keeps well, and its subtle flavors make it perfect for serving with midmorning coffee or late-afternoon tea. It also makes a lovely dessert when sliced very thin and served with softly whipped vanilla-flavored cream.

3 ounces semisweet chocolate, coarsely chopped

2 teaspoons instant espresso powder

1 cup warm water

1 1/2 cups all-purpose flour

2 teaspoons baking powder

1/2 teaspoon baking soda

1/4 teaspoon salt

1/2 cup (1 stick) unsalted butter, softened

1 1/4 cups sugar

2 large eggs

1 1/2 teaspoons pure vanilla extract

1/2 cup coarsely chopped pecans

Pecan halves, for decoration (optional)

Preheat the oven to 350°F. Grease an 8-by-4-by-3-inch loaf pan. Dust it with flour and tap out the excess.

Melt the chocolate in the top of a double boiler set over barely simmering (not boiling) water, stirring until smooth. Or microwave the chocolate in a microwave-safe container, uncovered, on medium (50 percent) power for 2 to 4 minutes, stirring once, until the chocolate is shiny; remove from the microwave and stir until smooth and melted. Set aside to cool to lukewarm.

In a small bowl, dissolve the espresso in the warm water.

In a medium bowl, whisk together the flour, baking powder, baking soda, and salt.

In a large bowl, using an electric mixer set at high, cream together the butter and sugar until light and fluffy. Add the eggs one at a time, beating well after each addition. Add the vanilla. Reduce the

mixer speed to low and beat in the cooled, melted chocolate. Alternately beat in the coffee and flour mixtures until well blended. Stir in the pecans.

Scrape the batter into the prepared pan and tap it on the counter to remove any air bubbles. Bake in the center of the oven for 60 to 70 minutes, or until the top springs back when pressed lightly and a skewer or toothpick inserted into the center comes out clean.

Set the pan on a wire rack to cool for 10 minutes. Using a knife, loosen the sides of the cake. Invert it onto the rack and cool completely. Transfer the cake to a serving plate, cut into thin slices, and decorate with pecan halves, if desired. **Serves 8 to 10.**

Devil's Food Cake with Sour Cream Fudge Frosting

The reaction between the nonalkalized cocoa powder and the baking soda gives this classic cake a reddish hue ~ and also its name. The cake is not overly sweet and makes a wonderful birthday cake when iced with the satiny fudge frosting.

Devil's Food Cake:

½ teaspoon instant espresso powder

1¾ cups warm water

1¾ cups cake flour

⅔ cup unsweetened nonalkalized cocoa powder

1½ teaspoons baking powder

1½ teaspoons baking soda

½ teaspoon salt

4 large eggs

1½ cups granulated sugar

2 teaspoons pure vanilla extract

10 tablespoons unsalted butter, melted

Sour Cream Fudge Frosting:

6 ounces unsweetened chocolate, coarsely chopped

3½ cups confectioners' sugar

½ cup sour cream

1 tablespoon pure vanilla extract

½ cup (1 stick) unsalted butter, softened

Prepare the cake: Preheat the oven to 350°F. Grease two 9-inch round cake pans and line the bottoms with parchment or waxed paper. Lightly grease the paper.

In a small bowl, dissolve the espresso in the warm water.

In a medium bowl, whisk together the flour, cocoa, baking powder, baking soda, and salt.

In a large bowl, using an electric mixer set at medium, beat together the eggs and sugar until smooth. Beat in the vanilla and melted butter. Alternately beat in the coffee and flour

mixtures until well blended. (The batter will be quite thin.)

Divide the batter evenly between the prepared pans and bake for 25 to 30 minutes, or until the tops spring back when pressed lightly and a skewer or toothpick inserted into the centers comes out clean.

Set the pans on wire racks to cool for 10 minutes. Using a knife, loosen the sides of the cakes. Invert the layers onto the wire racks, peel off the paper, and cool completely.

Prepare the frosting: Melt the chocolate in the top of a double boiler set over barely simmering (not boiling) water, stirring until smooth. Or microwave the chocolate in a microwave-safe container, uncovered, on medium (50 percent) power for 2 to 4 minutes, stirring once, until the chocolate is shiny; remove from the microwave and stir until smooth and melted. Set aside to cool to lukewarm.

In a medium bowl, using an electric mixer set at medium high, beat together the confectioners' sugar, sour cream, vanilla, and cooled melted chocolate until smooth. Add the softened butter 2 tablespoons at a time, beating until smooth and creamy after each addition.

Spread one third of the frosting over one of the cake layers. Top it with the other layer. Use the remaining frosting to frost the top and sides of the cake. For a smooth finish, dip a metal spatula in hot water, wipe it dry, and smooth it over the frosting. **Serves 8 to 10.**

Chocolate Sponge Roll with Orange Cream Filling

Cake rolls are surprisingly easy to make. The key to success is to roll the cake while it is still warm from the oven and then let it cool completely before unrolling it for filling. For serving, you will need a 16- to 18-inch rectangular platter or a large board covered with foil. Decorate the platter or board with paper doilies or lemon leaves, if desired.

Chocolate Sponge Roll:

⅓ cup cake flour

¼ cup unsweetened nonalkalized cocoa powder

3 tablespoons cornstarch

¼ teaspoon baking soda

⅛ teaspoon salt

5 large eggs, separated

¾ cup granulated sugar

2 teaspoons pure vanilla extract

Orange Cream Filling:

2 cups heavy cream, chilled

⅓ cup confectioners' sugar

1½ tablespoons orange-flavored liqueur

1 tablespoon grated orange zest

1 teaspoon pure vanilla extract

Thin strips orange peel, for decoration (optional)

Prepare the sponge roll: Preheat the oven to 350°F. Grease a 10-by-15-inch jelly-roll pan and line the bottom with parchment or waxed paper. Lightly grease the paper.

In a small bowl, whisk together the flour, cocoa, cornstarch, baking soda, and salt.

In a medium bowl, using an electric mixer set at high, beat the egg yolks with ¼ cup of the granulated sugar for 3 minutes, or until light and pale yellow. Beat in the vanilla.

In another medium bowl, using an electric mixer set at high, beat the egg whites with clean, dry beaters until soft

Packing Hershey's kisses, 1920s.

peaks form. Gradually add the remaining ½ cup sugar, and beat until smooth and glossy.

Stir about one third of the egg whites into the yolks to lighten them. Using a rubber spatula, gently and thoroughly fold in half the flour mixture and half the remaining egg whites. Repeat with the remaining flour and egg whites.

Spread the batter in the prepared pan. Bake in the center of the oven for 13 to 15 minutes, or until a skewer or toothpick inserted into the center comes out clean.

Dampen a kitchen towel and wring out as much water as possible. Using a knife, loosen the edges of the cake. Place the towel over the cake. Hold it in place and invert the cake onto the towel. Peel off the paper and, using a serrated knife, trim off any crisp edges of cake. Beginning with a long side, roll up the cake tightly in the towel. Let the cake cool in the towel, seam side down, on a wire rack.

Prepare the filling: In a chilled medium bowl, using an electric mixer set at high, beat the cream with the confectioners' sugar until stiff peaks form. Beat in the liqueur, zest, and vanilla.

Unroll the cake onto a work surface. Spread about one third of the filling over the cake, leaving a 1-inch border around the sides. Reroll the cake and place it seam side down on a serving platter. Frost the sides and top of the cake roll with the remaining cream. Insert toothpicks into the top of the cake, then loosely cover with plastic wrap, using the toothpicks to hold the plastic above the whipped cream. Chill for at least 2 hours or for up to 6 hours before serving. Decorate with orange peel, if desired. **Serves 8 to 10.**

Old-Fashioned Marble Pound Cake

*This simple loaf cake keeps well and is a great
idea for lunch box treats or picnics. For an extra-special dessert,
serve it with scoops of ice cream and hot fudge sauce.*

3 ounces semisweet chocolate,
  coarsely chopped

2 cups all-purpose flour

1 teaspoon baking powder

½ teaspoon salt

1 cup (2 sticks) unsalted butter,
  softened

1½ cups sugar

5 large eggs

1½ teaspoons pure vanilla
  extract

Preheat the oven to 325°F. Grease a 9-by-5-by-3-inch loaf pan. Dust it with flour and tap out the excess.

Melt the chocolate in the top of a double boiler set over barely simmering (not boiling) water, stirring until smooth. Or microwave the chocolate in a microwave-safe container, uncovered, on medium (50 percent) power for 2 to 4 minutes, stirring once, until the chocolate is shiny; remove from the microwave and stir until smooth and melted. Set aside to cool to lukewarm.

In a small bowl, whisk together the flour, baking powder, and salt.

In a large bowl, using an electric mixer set at high, cream together the butter and sugar until light and fluffy. Add the eggs one at a time, beating well after each addition. Add the vanilla and beat well. Reduce the mixer speed to low and beat in the flour mixture until just blended.

Transfer half the batter to a medium bowl. Add the melted chocolate and stir until well blended.

Spoon one third of the vanilla batter into the prepared pan. Smooth the top with a spatula or the back of a spoon. Spoon half the chocolate batter over the vanilla layer and smooth the top.

Repeat with the remaining batter so that you have three layers of vanilla and two of chocolate. (The top layer will be vanilla.) Insert a small metal spatula or table knife into the batter and gently swirl to create a marbled effect.

Bake in the center of the oven for 1 hour and 15 minutes, or until a skewer or toothpick inserted into the center comes out clean.

Set the pan on a wire rack to cool for 10 minutes. Using a knife, loosen the sides of the cake. Invert it onto the rack and cool completely. Transfer the cake to a serving plate. Serve at room temperature. **Serves 8 to 10.**

Chocolate Cream Pie

Luscious chocolate cream pie has been loved by generations of children ~ and their parents!

Chocolate Cookie Crust:

Approximately 30 plain chocolate cookie wafers

6 tablespoons unsalted butter, melted

Chocolate Filling:

¾ cup sugar

3 tablespoons cornstarch

2 tablespoons all-purpose flour

Pinch of salt

2 cups milk

1 cup half-and-half

4 large egg yolks

4 ounces semisweet chocolate, finely chopped

2 teaspoons pure vanilla extract

Chocolate Leaves:

10 ounces bittersweet or milk chocolate

24 non-toxic rose leaves

Whipped cream, for decoration

Prepare the crust: Preheat the oven to 350°F. In a food processor fitted with the metal blade, process the cookie wafers until finely ground. Or, using a rolling pin, crush the wafers between 2 pieces of waxed paper to make fine crumbs. You will have about 1½ cups crumbs.

In a small bowl, combine the crumbs and melted butter; stir until well blended. Using the palm of your hand, press the moistened crumbs into the bottom and up the sides of an ungreased 9-inch pie plate. Bake in the center of the oven for 7 to 8 minutes, or until the crust is set. Set on a wire rack to cool.

Prepare the filling: In a heavy medium-size saucepan, combine the sugar, cornstarch, flour, salt, milk, and half-and-half. Cook, stirring frequently, over medium heat until the mixture is hot but

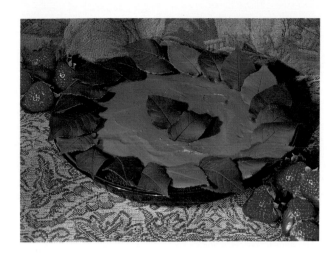

not boiling. Remove the pan from the heat.

In a small bowl, lightly beat the egg yolks. Stir about ¼ cup of the hot milk mixture into the yolks to temper them. Return this mixture to the saucepan of hot milk. Cook, whisking constantly, for 3 to 4 minutes, or until the mixture is thick but not boiling.

Put the chocolate in a medium bowl and pour the hot milk mixture over it. Let stand for 30 seconds, then stir until smooth and melted. Cool for 15 minutes. Stir in the vanilla.

Pour the filling into the baked pie crust. Place plastic wrap directly on the surface of the filling and cool to room temperature. Chill for 3 to 4 hours or overnight.

Prepare the leaves: Wash and thoroughly dry the leaves. Melt the chocolate. Spoon or brush it about ¹⁄₁₆ inch thick onto the back of each leaf. (Do not spread the chocolate to the edges.) Chill the chocolate-coated leaves for 20 to 30 minutes, or until the chocolate is set. Beginning at the stem end, gently peel the leaf from the chocolate. Chill the leaves until ready to use.

Decorate the pie with chocolate leaves and whipped cream. **Serves 8 to 10.**

Mississippi Mud Pie

So named because the thick, dark filling with its cracked top resembles the rich mud of our most famous river, Mississippi mud pie claims legions of chocolate fans. And for good reason: There is nothing subtle about the dessert. It is a pure, unadulterated, intense chocolate experience.

Sweet Pastry Crust:

1 cup all-purpose flour

2 teaspoons sugar

¼ teaspoon salt

¼ cup (½ stick) unsalted butter, chilled & cut into small pieces

2 tablespoons solid vegetable shortening, chilled & cut into small pieces

2 to 3 tablespoons ice water

Chocolate Filling:

2 ounces unsweetened chocolate, coarsely chopped

1 ounce semisweet chocolate, coarsely chopped

½ cup (1 stick) unsalted butter

2 teaspoons instant espresso powder

3 large eggs

1 cup plus 2 tablespoons sugar

¼ cup light corn syrup

1½ teaspoons pure vanilla extract

Prepare the crust: In a small bowl, combine the flour, sugar, and salt. Using your fingertips, 2 knives, or a pastry blender, cut the butter and shortening into the flour until the mixture resembles coarse meal. Sprinkle the mixture with the ice water. Mix with a fork, then add enough additional water to gather the dough into a ball. Flatten it into a disk, wrap in plastic, and chill for at least 1 hour or up to 2 days. (Alternatively, in a food processor fitted with the metal blade, process the flour, sugar, and salt briefly. Add the butter and shortening and process by pulsing on and off until the mixture resembles coarse meal. With the machine running, drizzle the ice water

through the feed tube, stopping the motor when the dough begins to gather into a ball. Scrape the dough from the work bowl, shape it into a ball, and flatten into a disk. Wrap in plastic and chill as directed.)

Remove the dough from the refrigerator and let it stand for about 10 minutes before rolling. Roll it out on a lightly floured surface into an 11-inch round. Transfer to a 9-inch pie plate and press it into the bottom and up the side. Trim and flute the edges. Freeze until ready to fill. (Freezing relaxes the gluten in the flour and reduces shrinking during baking.)

Prepare the filling: Preheat the oven to 350°F. Melt both chocolates with the butter and espresso in the top of a double boiler set over barely simmering (not boiling) water, stirring until smooth. Or microwave the mixture in a microwave-safe container, covered loosely with waxed paper, on medium (50 percent) power for 2 to 4 minutes, stirring once, until the chocolate is shiny and the butter is melted; remove from the microwave and stir until smooth. Set aside to cool slightly.

In a medium bowl, whisk together the eggs, sugar, corn syrup, and vanilla. Whisk in the chocolate mixture. Pour the filling into the prepared pie crust. Bake in the lower third of the oven for 40 to 45 minutes, or until the filling puffs up and the top is deeply cracked and slightly crisp. Set the pie on a wire rack to cool. The filling will sink during cooling. Serve at room temperature. **Serves 6 to 8.**

NOTE: To make a decorative crust, prepare an additional half recipe of the sweet pastry. Roll out the dough to a $\frac{1}{8}$-inch thickness. Using a sharp knife, cut out small leaf shapes. Make veins by pressing the back of the knife into the leaves. Fill the pie crust, then arrange the leaves around the edges. Brush with lightly beaten egg white and bake as directed.

Black Bottom Pie

Like so many wonderful old-fashioned pies, this one originated in the South. Classic black bottom pie is made from two layers of custard nestled in a gingersnap or graham cracker crust and seductively flavored with chocolate and rum. In this simplified version, the custard is thickened with egg yolks and cornstarch rather than with gelatin.

Gingersnap Crust:

Approximately 35 small
    gingersnaps

6 tablespoons unsalted
    butter, melted

Black and White Custard Filling:

¾ cup granulated sugar

2 tablespoons cornstarch

¼ teaspoon salt

2½ cups milk

3 large egg yolks

5 ounces semisweet chocolate,
    coarsely chopped

2 tablespoons unsalted
    butter, softened

2 tablespoons dark rum

1 teaspoon pure vanilla extract

Rum Cream Topping:

¾ cup heavy cream

3 tablespoons confectioners'
    sugar

1 tablespoon dark rum

1 block semisweet, bittersweet,
    milk or white chocolate, for
    chocolate shavings (optional)

Prepare the crust: Preheat the oven to 350°F. In a food processor fitted with the metal blade, process the gingersnaps until finely ground. Or, using a rolling pin, crush the cookies between 2 pieces of waxed paper to make fine crumbs. You will have about 1½ cups crumbs.

In a small bowl, combine the crumbs and melted butter; stir until well blended. Using the palm of your hand, press the moistened crumbs into the bottom and up the sides of an ungreased 9-inch pie

plate. Bake in the center of the oven for 7 to 8 minutes, or until the crust turns a deep golden brown. Set the pie crust on a wire rack to cool.

Prepare the filling: In a heavy medium-size saucepan, combine the sugar, cornstarch, and salt. Add ½ cup milk and whisk until smooth. Add the remaining milk and the egg yolks and whisk until smooth. Set the saucepan over medium-high heat and whisk constantly until the custard comes to a boil. Still whisking, boil for 1 minute. Remove the pan from the heat.

In a small bowl, combine 1 cup of the hot custard and the chopped chocolate; stir until smooth. Pour this mixture into the cooled pie crust and smooth it over the bottom.

Add the butter to the warm custard remaining in the saucepan and stir until melted. Stir in the vanilla and rum. Gently pour this mixture over the chocolate custard.

Chill the pie for 1 hour, or until firm.

Prepare the topping: In a medium bowl, using an electric mixer set at high, beat the cream with the confectioners' sugar until stiff peaks form. Beat in the rum. Spread the cream evenly over the chilled pie.

To make the shavings: Using a sharp vegetable peeler, shave strips from chocolate. The chocolate block should be soft enough to scrape but firm enough so the curls hold their shape. Sprinkle over the pie, if desired. Serve chilled. **Serves 8 to 10.**

NOTE: The pie crust can be baked a day ahead of serving. Wrap in plastic and store in the refrigerator. There is no need to bring it to room temperature before spreading the chocolate layer in it. The pie can be assembled 3 or 4 hours before serving. Cover loosely with plastic and refrigerate.

Bourbon Chocolate-Pecan Pie

*Because buttery pecans thrive in the Deep South, pecan pie is
a natural outgrowth of the region. Recipes for this all-American classic
vary only slightly from county to county and state and state,
and many are dressed up, as this one is, with bourbon and chocolate.
Serve it warm with vanilla ice cream or whipped cream.*

Pastry Crust:

1 cup all-purpose flour

¼ teaspoon salt

¼ cup (½ stick) unsalted butter,
chilled & cut into small pieces

2 tablespoons solid vegetable
shortening, chilled &
cut into small pieces

2 to 3 tablespoons ice water

Bourbon Chocolate-Pecan Filling:

3 large eggs

¾ cup packed light brown sugar

⅔ cup dark corn syrup

¼ cup (½ stick) unsalted
butter, melted

¼ teaspoon salt

2 tablespoons bourbon

1 teaspoon pure vanilla extract

4½ ounces (¾ cup) semisweet
chocolate chips

1 cup pecan halves

Prepare the crust: In a small bowl, combine the flour and salt. Using your fingertips, 2 knives, or a pastry blender, cut the butter and shortening into the flour until the mixture resembles coarse meal. Sprinkle the mixture with 2 tablespoons ice water. Mix with a fork, then add enough of the remaining water to gather the dough into a ball. Flatten it into a disk, wrap in plastic, and chill for at least 1 hour or up to 2 days. (Alternatively, in a food processor fitted with the metal blade, process the flour and salt briefly. Add the butter and shortening, and process by pulsing on and off until the mixture resembles coarse meal. With the machine running, drizzle the ice water through the feed tube, stopping the motor when the dough begins to gather into a ball. Scrape the dough from the work bowl, shape it into a ball, and flatten into a disk. Wrap in plastic and chill as directed.)

Remove the dough from the refrigerator and let it stand for about 10 minutes before rolling. Roll it out on a lightly floured surface into an 11-inch round, then transfer it to a 9-inch pie plate and press it into the bottom and up the sides. Trim and flute the edges. Freeze the pie crust until ready to fill. (Freezing relaxes the gluten in the flour and reduces shrinking during baking.)

Prepare the filling: Preheat the oven to 375°F. In a medium bowl, whisk together the eggs, sugar, corn syrup, butter, and salt. Whisk in the bourbon and vanilla.

Spread the chocolate chips in an even layer over the bottom of the prepared pie crust. Sprinkle the pecans evenly over the chocolate. Pour the filling into the pie crust. The nuts will rise to the surface and may need redistributing.

Bake in the lower third of the oven for 35 to 45 minutes, or until a knife inserted two thirds of the way into the center comes out clean. The filling will be semifirm in the middle and quiver slightly when the pie is gently shaken. Set the pie on a wire rack to cool completely. Serve at room temperature. **Serves 10.**

NOTE: The dough can be made ahead of time and frozen for up to 1 month well wrapped in plastic, then foil. The pie can be baked several hours before serving and stored, loosely covered, at room temperature or in the refrigerator. If chilled, let it return to room temperature before serving.

Chunky Chocolate Peanut Pie

The combination of chocolate and peanuts is almost an American institution, and for a delicious reason. For more chocolate clout, substitute the chocolate cookie crust on page 48 for the graham cracker crust here.

Graham Cracker Crust:

12 to 14 whole graham crackers

6 tablespoons unsalted butter, melted

Dark Chocolate Layer:

¾ cup heavy cream

4 ounces semisweet chocolate, coarsely chopped

Peanut Mousse Filling:

½ cup sugar

1½ tablespoons cornstarch

⅛ teaspoon salt

1½ cups milk

2 large egg yolks

1 teaspoon pure vanilla extract

¾ cup chunky or extra-chunky peanut butter

Whipped cream, for decoration (optional)

2 tablespoons chopped toasted peanuts, for decoration (optional)

Prepare the crust: Preheat the oven to 350°F. In a food processor fitted with the metal blade, process the graham crackers until finely ground. Or, using a rolling pin, crush the crackers between 2 pieces of waxed paper to make fine crumbs. You will have about 1½ cups crumbs.

In a small bowl, combine the crumbs and butter; stir until well blended. Using the palm of your hand, press the moistened crumbs into the bottom and up the sides of an ungreased 9-inch pie plate. Bake in the center of the oven for 7 to 8 minutes, or until the crust darkens in color. Set the pie crust on a wire rack to cool.

Prepare the chocolate layer: In a small saucepan, heat the cream over medium heat until small bubbles appear around the

edges. Remove the pan from the heat, add the chocolate, and stir until melted and smooth. Pour the mixture into the cooled pie crust, smoothing it over the bottom. Freeze for 30 to 40 minutes, or until the chocolate layer is firm.

Prepare the mousse: In a heavy medium-size saucepan, combine the sugar, cornstarch, and salt. Add ½ cup milk and whisk until smooth. Add the remaining milk and the egg yolks and whisk until smooth. Set the saucepan over medium-high heat and whisk constantly until the custard comes to a boil. Still whisking, boil for 1 minute. Remove the pan from the heat and stir in the vanilla and peanut butter. Pour the mousse into the baked pie crust. Chill for 1 hour, or until firm. Before serving, decorate the pie with whipped cream and sprinkle with the chopped peanuts, if desired. **Serves 8 to 10.**

NOTE: The pie crust can be made a day ahead of serving. Wrap in plastic and store it in the refrigerator. There is no need to bring it to room temperature before spreading with the chocolate layer. The pie can be assembled up to 8 hours before serving. Cover loosely with plastic and refrigerate.

Chocolate Raspberry Tarts with Nut Crust

If you prefer, make a large tart rather than four
individual tartlets, using a 9-inch tart pan. It will serve 4 to 6.

Nut Crust:

¼ cup slivered almonds

¾ cup all-purpose flour

1 tablespoon sugar

¼ teaspoon salt

6 tablespoons unsalted butter,
  chilled & cut into small pieces

1 large egg yolk

2 to 3 tablespoons ice water

Chocolate Raspberry Filling:

5 ounces semisweet chocolate,
  coarsely chopped

1 pint raspberries

2 tablespoons raspberry or red
  currant jelly

1 tablespoon raspberry brandy,
  (framboise), or water

Prepare the crust: In a food processor fitted with the metal blade, process the almonds with 2 tablespoons of the flour until finely ground. Take care the nuts do not turn to paste. Add the remaining flour, the sugar, and salt, and process until blended. Add the butter and process by pulsing on and off until the mixture resembles coarse meal. In a small bowl, whisk the egg yolk with 2 tablespoons ice water. With the motor running, pour the egg mixture through the feed tube, and process until the dough begins to gather into a ball. Add the remaining tablespoon of water only if the dough is too dry to form a cohesive mass. Scrape the dough from the work bowl, shape it into a ball and flatten it into a disk. Wrap in plastic wrap and chill for at least 1 hour, or up to 2 days.

Remove the dough from the refrigerator and let it stand for about 10 minutes. Divide the dough into 4 equal pieces. Using your fingers and the heel

of your hand, press the dough into four 4- to 4½-inch mini tart pans, preferably with removable bottoms. The crust will be about ¼ inch thick. Freeze for at least 15 minutes, or until ready to bake. (Freezing relaxes the gluten in the flour and reduces the shrinking during baking.)

Preheat the oven to 400°F. Bake the tart shells in the lower third of the oven for about 12 minutes, or until they start to brown. If the shells puff up during baking, use your hand to flatten them. Reduce the oven temperature to 350°F and bake for another 15 minutes, or until the pastry turns golden brown. Set the tart shells on wire racks to cool.

Prepare the filling: Melt the chocolate in the top of a double boiler set over barely simmering (not boiling) water, stirring until smooth. Or microwave the chocolate in a microwave-safe container, uncovered, on medium (50 percent) power for 2 to 4 minutes, stirring once, until the chocolate is shiny; remove from the microwave and stir until smooth and melted.

Divide the melted chocolate evenly among the cooled tart shells, spreading it evenly over the bottom of each one. Let the chocolate set for about 15 minutes. Then arrange the raspberries in the tart shells so that they cover the chocolate completely. Refrigerate the tarts for about 20 minutes, or until the chocolate is completely set.

In a small saucepan, combine the jelly and liqueur. Cook over low heat, stirring occasionally, for about 1 minute, or until the jelly melts and the mixture is smooth. Gently brush the raspberries with the glaze. Serve immediately, or store at room temperature for up to 8 hours. **Serves 4.**

NOTE: The dough can be made ahead of time and frozen for up to 1 month if well wrapped in plastic, then foil.

Old-Fashioned Chocolate Pudding

Setting plastic wrap directly on the surface of the pudding as it cools prevents a thin skin from forming. If you like the skin, however, stretch the plastic wrap over the top of the custard cups so that it does not touch the pudding.

½ cup sugar

2 tablespoons cornstarch

⅛ teaspoon salt

1 cup milk

1 cup half-and-half

3 large egg yolks

3 ounces semisweet chocolate, finely chopped

2 teaspoons pure vanilla extract

Whipped cream (optional)

In a heavy medium-size saucepan, combine the sugar, cornstarch, salt, milk, and half-and-half. Cook, whisking frequently, over medium heat until the mixture is hot but not boiling. Remove the pan from the heat.

In a small bowl, lightly beat the egg yolks. Stir about ¼ cup of the hot milk mixture into the yolks to temper them. Return this mixture to the saucepan with the hot milk. Cook, whisking constantly, for 3 to 4 minutes, or until the mixture is thick but not boiling.

Put the chocolate in a medium bowl and pour the hot milk mixture over it. Let stand for about 30 seconds, then stir until smooth and melted. Cool for 10 to 15 minutes. Stir in the vanilla.

Pour the pudding into four 6-ounce ramekins or custard cups. Place plastic wrap directly on the surface of the pudding and cool to room temperature. Chill for 3 to 4 hours or overnight. Serve the pudding chilled or at room temperature, with whipped cream, if desired. **Serves 4.**

Mocha Pots de Crème

*These silken desserts, a lovely cross between a mousse
and a pudding, stand in a class by themselves.*

2 cups milk

6 ounces semisweet chocolate,
coarsely chopped

1 tablespoon instant espresso
powder

6 large egg yolks

⅓ cup sugar

2 teaspoons pure vanilla extract

Whipped cream, for decoration
(optional)

Chocolate-covered espresso
beans, for decoration
(optional)

Preheat the oven to 325°F. In a heavy medium-size saucepan, combine ⅔ cup of the milk with the chocolate and espresso. Cook, stirring frequently, over medium heat until the chocolate melts. Stir in the remaining 1⅓ cups milk and remove the pan from the heat.

In a medium bowl, whisk together the egg yolks and sugar until light and slightly thickened. Slowly whisk in the warm chocolate milk mixture. Stir in the vanilla.

Pour the custard into six 6-ounce ramekins, custard cups, or pots de crème cups with lids. Cover the ramekins or custard cups with foil, or set the lids on the pots de crème cups. Put the cups in a large baking pan and add enough hot water to the pan to come halfway up the sides of the cups. Bake in the water bath in the center of the oven for 40 to 45 minutes, or until the custard is softly set. (It won't be firm.)

Remove the cups from the water bath, uncover, and set on wire racks to cool. Then cover the cups and chill for at least 1 hour, or until cold. Decorate the pots de crème with whipped cream and espresso beans, if desired. Serve chilled. **Serves 6.**

White Chocolate Mousse and Strawberry Parfaits

*This stunningly pretty, do-ahead dessert is
wonderfully light and refreshing and just right for a warm-weather
chocolate indulgence. Use firm ripe berries for the strawberry
sauce and cream-colored real white chocolate for the mousse. If the chocolate
is bright white or labeled "confectionery" or "summer coating,"
it may not be white chocolate; read the label to ascertain that it is
made with cocoa butter, not vegetable fat.*

Strawberry Sauce:

1½ pints strawberries

¼ cup sugar

1½ tablespoons cherry-flavored
  liqueur (kirsch)

1 teaspoon fresh lemon juice

White Chocolate Mousse:

1 cup heavy cream

6 ounces white chocolate,
  coarsely chopped

White Chocolate Curls, for
  decoration (p.37, optional)

Mint leaves, for decoration
  (optional)

Prepare the sauce: Set aside the 6 largest, prettiest strawberries for decoration. Remove the stems from the remaining berries and slice half of them. Set the sliced berries aside.

In a food processor fitted with the metal blade, process the remaining berries with the sugar until pureed.

In a small saucepan, combine the berry puree with the sliced berries. Bring to a boil over medium-high heat, stirring frequently, and boil for 2 minutes. Remove the pan from the heat and stir in the liqueur and lemon juice. Transfer the sauce to a small bowl and set aside to cool slightly, stirring occasionally. Chill the sauce for at least 1 hour, or until cold.

Prepare the mousse: In a small saucepan, heat $\frac{1}{4}$ cup of the cream over medium heat until small bubbles form around the edges. Remove the pan from the heat, add the chocolate, and stir until it is melted and smooth. If necessary, set the pan over very low heat to help melt the chocolate. Transfer to a medium bowl and chill, stirring occasionally, for 20 to 30 minutes, or until the mixture is cool (about 65°F) and thick.

In a small bowl, using an electric mixer set at high, beat the remaining $\frac{3}{4}$ cup cream until stiff peaks form. Stir about one fourth of the whipped cream into the chilled chocolate mixture to lighten it. Using a rubber spatula, gen-tly and thoroughly fold in the remaining whipped cream.

Spoon half the cold strawberry sauce into 6 parfait glasses or 8-ounce stemmed goblets. Spoon half the white choco-late mousse evenly over the sauce. Repeat with the remaining sauce and mousse. Cover the glasses with plastic wrap and chill for at least 1 hour. When ready to serve, decorate each parfait with white chocolate curls and mint leaves, if desired. **Serves 6.**

NOTE: Both the strawberry sauce and the mousse can be made 1 day ahead of time. Store them separately in airtight containers in the refrigerator. Assemble the parfaits an hour or so before serving.

Chocolate Mousse with Candied Orange Threads

Traditionally, mousses are made with uncooked egg whites. This one avoids eggs by relying instead on milk to lighten the base and a little vegetable oil to smooth the texture. The result is light and satiny. This recipe is adapted from one developed by Adrienne Welch for her book, Unbelievable Microwave Desserts.

Chocolate Mousse:

½ cup milk

2 tablespoons sugar

1 teaspoon instant coffee powder

7 ounces semisweet chocolate, coarsely chopped

2 tablespoons vegetable oil

1 tablespoon pure vanilla extract

1 tablespoon orange-flavored liqueur

1 cup heavy cream, chilled

Candied Orange Threads:

2 oranges, rinsed

2 tablespoons water

6 tablespoons sugar

Whipped cream, for decoration (optional)

Prepare the mousse: In a heavy medium-size saucepan, combine the milk, sugar, and coffee. Cook, stirring frequently, over medium heat until the sugar dissolves. Add the chocolate and stir over low heat until the chocolate melts and the mixture is smooth.

Remove the pan from the heat and stir in the oil, vanilla, and liqueur. Pour the mixture into a large bowl, cover with plastic wrap, and chill for about 20 minutes, or until cool to the touch.

Stir the mixture occasionally.

In a medium bowl, using an electric mixer set at high, beat the cream to soft peaks. Stir about one third of the whipped cream into the chilled chocolate mixture to lighten it. Using a rubber spatula, gently and thoroughly fold in the remaining whipped cream. Don't worry if a few streaks of white remain.

Transfer the mousse to a glass serving bowl or spoon it into 4 or 5 stemmed goblets or serving dishes. Cover with plastic wrap and chill for at least 30 minutes, or until set.

Prepare the orange threads: Using a zester or a small sharp knife, cut 3 tablespoons of zest from the oranges. In a heavy small-size saucepan, combine the water with 4 tablespoons of the sugar. Cook over medium-high heat, stirring constantly, until the sugar dissolves. Let the syrup boil, uncovered, for 1 minute. Add the orange zest, separating them with a fork. Cook, without stirring, for about 3 minutes, or until the syrup begins to turn a light caramel color around the edges.

Remove the pan from the heat.

Put the remaining 2 tablespoons sugar in a small, shallow bowl. Lift the threads from the syrup with a fork and toss them in the sugar. Use your fingers to separate them so that each thread is coated with sugar. They will cool almost immediately. Discard any remaining sugar.

To serve, spoon whipped cream over the mousse, if desired, and sprinkle with the candied orange threads. **Serves 4 to 5.**

NOTE: The mousse can be made 8 hours ahead of time, covered with plastic wrap, and refrigerated.

Double-Chocolate Mousse: Prepare the Chocolate Mousse as directed. Prepare White Chocolate Mousse according to the recipe on p. 66. Spoon about 1 inch of chocolate mousse into the bottom of each of 8 to 10 parfait or stemmed glasses. Spoon about 1 inch of white chocolate mousse over the chocolate. Repeat the layers until the glasses are full. Cover with plastic wrap and chill for at least 1 hour, or until ready to serve. **Serves 8 to 10.**

Chocolate Pan Soufflé

This soufflé puffs up proudly every time because it is baked in a shallow dish and does not have to climb as high as those baked in traditional soufflé dishes. But the differences stop there: Once mixed with the egg whites, the base must be baked right away, and the baked soufflé served immediately, or it will collapse. Leftovers, however, still taste good and have the texture of light chocolate pudding.

2 tablespoons unsalted butter

2 tablespoons all-purpose flour

⅔ cup milk

⅛ teaspoon salt

3 large eggs, separated

4 ounces semisweet chocolate, coarsely chopped

2 teaspoons pure vanilla extract

2 large egg whites

⅓ cup granulated sugar

Confectioners' sugar for dusting (optional)

Whipped cream, for decoration (optional)

In a heavy medium-size saucepan, melt the butter over medium heat. Stir in the flour and cook, stirring constantly, for 2 minutes. Increase the heat to medium-high, stir in the milk, and bring to a boil. Cook, stirring constantly, for 1 minute. Stir in the salt, and remove the pan from the heat.

Add the egg yolks one at a time to the hot milk mixture, stirring well after each addition. Add the chocolate and stir until the chocolate melts and the mixture is smooth. Stir in the vanilla. Transfer the mixture to a medium bowl and cool for 10 to 15 minutes, or until lukewarm.

Preheat the oven to 425°F. Generously grease a 10-inch pie plate or shallow baking dish of similar capacity. Sprinkle the pie plate or dish with granulated sugar.

In a medium bowl, using an electric mixer set at medium, beat the 5 egg whites until soft peaks form. Add the

granulated sugar and beat until the whites are shiny and stiff peaks form.

Stir about one fourth of the egg whites into the chocolate base to lighten it. Using a rubber spatula, gently and thoroughly fold in the remaining whites so that no streaks of white remain. Scrape the mixture into the pie plate. It will be full.

Bake in the center of the oven for 12 to 14 minutes, or until the soufflé puffs up evenly, the edges are firm, and the center is still wobbly. Remove from the oven and sprinkle with confectioners' sugar and whipped cream, if desired. Serve immediately. **Serves 4 to 5.**

NOTE: The chocolate base for the soufflé can be made up to 2 hours ahead of time and kept at cool room temperature. Place a piece of plastic wrap directly on the surface to prevent a skin from forming.

Cocoa-Dusted Mocha Truffles

Some truffles are covered with a shiny sheath of tempered chocolate.
These are much simpler to make because they require only a coating of cocoa.

6 ounces semisweet chocolate,
    coarsely chopped

3 tablespoons heavy cream

1 teaspoon instant coffee
    powder

2 tablespoons coffee-flavored
    liqueur (Kahlúa)

¼ cup (½ stick) unsalted
    butter, softened

¼ cup unsweetened
    nonalkalized cocoa powder

Melt the chocolate with the cream and coffee in the top of a double boiler set over barely simmering (not boiling) water, stirring until smooth. Or microwave the mixture in a microwave-safe container, uncovered, on medium (50 percent) power for 2 to 4 minutes, stirring once, until the chocolate is shiny; remove from the microwave and stir until smooth and melted. Stir in the liqueur. Add the butter 1 tablespoon at a time, beating until smooth after each addition.

Chill the mixture, stirring several times, for 25 to 40 minutes, or until it is firm enough to shape.

Line a baking sheet with plastic wrap. Sift the cocoa powder onto a plate or into a shallow pie tin. Using about 2 teaspoons of the chocolate mixture for each truffle, roll it into balls between the palms of your hands. Using your fingertips or 2 forks, quickly roll each ball in the cocoa power to coat. Set each truffle on the prepared baking sheet as it is coated.

Chill the truffles until firm. **Makes about 20 truffles.**

NOTE: The truffles will keep for 3 to 4 days if stored in the refrigerator in an airtight container between layers of waxed paper.

Toasted Macadamia Truffles

*This recipe combines salted macadamia nuts with sweet chocolate.
If you prefer, you can rinse and dry the nuts to rid them of salt, or buy
unsalted macadamias. Toasting the nuts brings out their flavor.*

6 ounces semisweet chocolate, coarsely chopped

3 tablespoons heavy cream

2 tablespoons brandy

¼ cup (½ stick) unsalted butter, softened

½ cup salted macadamia nuts, toasted & finely chopped

Melt the chocolate with the cream in the top of a double boiler set over barely simmering (not boiling) water, stirring until smooth. Or microwave the mixture in a microwave-safe container, uncovered, on medium (50 percent) power for 2 to 4 minutes, stirring once, until the chocolate is shiny; remove from the microwave and stir until smooth and melted. Stir in the brandy. Add the butter 1 tablespoon at a time, beating until smooth after each addition.

Chill the mixture, stirring several times, for 25 to 40 minutes, or until it is firm enough to shape.

Line a baking sheet with plastic wrap. Spread the chopped nuts on a plate or in a shallow pie tin. Using about 2 teaspoons of the chocolate mixture for each truffle, roll it into balls between the palms of your hands. Using your fingertips or 2 forks, quickly roll each ball in the chopped nuts to coat. Set each truffle on the prepared baking sheet as it is coated.

Chill the truffles until firm. **Makes about 20 truffles.**

NOTE: The truffles will keep for 3 to 4 days if stored in the refrigerator in an airtight container between layers of waxed paper.

Easy White Chocolate Fudge

This sweet, creamy fudge is custom-made for fans of white chocolate. It is easy to prepare and relies on marshmallow cream to make it silky smooth and fail-safe.

½ cup heavy cream

¾ cup sugar

1 tablespoon unsalted butter

¼ teaspoon salt

6 ounces white chocolate, coarsely chopped, or 6 ounces (1 cup) white chocolate chips

¾ cup marshmallow cream

½ cup chopped walnuts

1 teaspoon pure vanilla extract

Lightly grease an 8-inch square baking pan. In a heavy medium-size saucepan, bring the cream, sugar, butter, and salt to a boil over medium heat, stirring constantly until the sugar dissolves. Cover the saucepan and boil over medium-low heat for 1 minute to dissolve any sugar crystals on the sides of the pan. Do not stir.

Uncover the pan and cook for 5 minutes, stirring frequently to prevent scorching. Remove the pan from the heat and add the white chocolate and marshmallow cream.

Stir with a wooden spoon until the chocolate is melted and the mixture is smooth. Stir in the nuts and vanilla.

Scrape the fudge into the prepared pan and smooth the top. Chill for at least 1 hour, or until firm. Before the fudge sets completely, cut it into 25 large or 36 small squares.

NOTE: The fudge will keep for up to 1 week if stored in a cool place in an airtight container between layers of waxed paper.

Classic Fudge

Homemade fudge has a bold chocolate flavor and melt-in-the-mouth texture. This smoothness is almost unattainable without a good beating with a sturdy wooden spoon after cooking before the fudge mixture is set. Making fudge requires an accurate candy thermometer and some patience.

2 cups sugar

¾ cup half-and-half

3 tablespoons light corn syrup

3 ounces unsweetened chocolate, coarsely chopped

1 tablespoon unsalted butter, cut into small pieces

2 teaspoons pure vanilla extract

1 cup chopped walnuts (optional)

Lightly grease an 8-inch square baking pan. In a heavy medium-size saucepan, combine the sugar, half-and-half, and corn syrup. Bring to a boil over medium-high heat, stirring constantly until the sugar dissolves. Reduce the heat to low, add the chocolate, and cook, stirring constantly, for 1 minute, or until the chocolate melts. The mixture will be grainy.

Cover the saucepan and boil over medium-low heat for 2 minutes to dissolve any sugar crystals on the sides of the pan. Do not stir.

Uncover the pan and hang a candy thermometer over the side of the pan so that the tip is submerged in the boiling chocolate but is not touching the bottom of the pan. Cook over low heat without stirring for 30 minutes, or until the thermometer reaches 234°F (soft-ball stage). Remove the candy thermometer and wash it in hot water.

Remove the pan from the heat and set it in a cool place. Distribute the butter over the top of the fudge without jostling it. Insert the candy thermometer again and let the fudge cool for 35 to 45 minutes until lukewarm, or until the thermometer registers 110°F. Do not stir the fudge during this time.

When the fudge is cool, add the vanilla and beat with a wooden spoon for 5 to 10 minutes, or until the fudge loses its shine, thickens, and becomes nearly too stiff to beat. Stir in the walnuts, if desired.

Scrape the fudge into the prepared pan and smooth the top. Cool at room temperature for about 1 hour, or until firm. Before the fudge sets completely, cut it into 20 or 25 squares.

NOTE: The fudge will keep for up to 1 week if stored in a cool place in an airtight container between layers of waxed paper. Do not refrigerate.

Dark Chocolate-Covered Strawberries

*Chocolate-dipped strawberries look sophisticated and elegant,
yet are astonishingly easy to make. Use them to decorate dessert platters or cakes,
or serve them alone for dessert. The same method works for bananas, pineapple
chunks, and tangerine wedges. Use a toothpick to dip fruits without stems.*

3 ounces (½ cup) semisweet
chocolate chips

1 teaspoon vegetable oil
1 pint large strawberries

Line a baking sheet with plastic wrap. Melt the chocolate in the top of a double boiler set over barely simmering (not boiling) water, stirring until smooth. Or microwave the chocolate separately in microwave-safe containers, uncovered, on medium (50 percent) power for 1 to 2 minutes, stirring once, until the chocolate is shiny. Add the oil to the chocolate and stir until smooth and melted.

Dip the strawberries, one at a time, in the chocolate so that the chocolate covers them about halfway. Let any excess chocolate drip back into the containers.

Lay the strawberries on the prepared baking sheet and chill for about 15 minutes, or until the chocolate is set. Serve immediately or refrigerate for up to 8 hours. **Serves 6 to 8.**

Black and White Ice Cream Soda

*A traditional black-and-white soda is made with creamy
vanilla ice cream, but there is no reason you can't experiment with different
flavors ~ coffee or strawberry would be delicious, or a scoop of vanilla
and a scoop of chocolate. For the most authenticity and best foam, use seltzer from
a siphon. Set the soda glass on a plate to catch the frothy overflow.*

⅓ cup chocolate syrup

2 scoops vanilla ice cream

Soda water

Whipped cream, for decoration
(optional)

Put the chocolate syrup in the bottom of a chilled tall glass. Top with 1 scoop of ice cream. Fill the glass with soda water and then add the other scoop of ice cream. (The soda water will overflow a little.) Top with whipped cream, if desired. Serve with a straw and a long spoon. **Serves 1.**

Hot Chocolate

Few hot drinks are as soothing as a steaming mug of old-fashioned cocoa, and it really tastes best when made with whole milk, unsweetened cocoa, and sugar. The whipped cream is a delicious decoration, but not necessary for chocolate satisfaction. Double, triple, or quadruple the recipe as needed.

1 cup whole milk
1 ½ teaspoons unsweetened nonalkalized cocoa powder
1 tablespoon sugar

Whipped cream, for decoration (optional)
Chocolate Shavings, for decoration (p. 55, optional)

In a small saucepan, heat the milk over medium heat until hot but not bubbling. Stir in the cocoa and sugar until dissolved, taking care the milk does not boil. Remove the pan from the heat. Or microwave the milk in a small microwave-safe container, covered loosely with waxed paper, on medium (50 percent) power for 1 ½ minutes. Stir in the cocoa and sugar and microwave, covered, on medium-high (70 percent) power for 35 to 40 seconds, or until hot but not boiling; stir well.

Pour the hot chocolate into a large mug. Top with whipped cream and chocolate shavings, if desired. **Serves 1.**

White Hot Chocolate

Velvety smooth and sinfully rich, white hot chocolate is sweet
ambrosia to white chocolate lovers. Heat the mixture gently; white chocolate
warrants special treatment because it is very heat-sensitive.

1 cup whole milk

1 ½ ounces white chocolate,
   finely chopped

1 teaspoon pure vanilla extract

Whipped cream (optional)

Pinch of cinnamon (optional)

In a small saucepan, combine the milk, white chocolate, and vanilla. Cook over medium-low heat, stirring occasionally, until hot but not bubbling. Remove the pan from the heat. Or microwave the milk in a small microwave-safe container, covered loosely with waxed paper, on medium (50 percent) power for 1 minute. Stir in the white chocolate and vanilla, and microwave, covered, on medium (50 percent) power for 1 minute more. Stir well, then cover and microwave on medium-high (70 percent) power for 30 to 45 seconds, or until hot but not boiling.

Pour the hot chocolate into a large mug. Top with whipped cream and sprinkle with cinnamon, if desired. **Serves 1.**

Chocolate shop interior, Brussels.

Rum-Chocolate Espresso

This powerful, sweet hot drink packs a pleasant punch after a day on the ski slopes or pursuing other outdoor wintertime activities. Rum, crème de cacao, and espresso make this a very adult version of cocoa.

¼ cup hot freshly brewed espresso or strong coffee

¾ cup Hot Chocolate (p. 74)

2 tablespoons dark rum

1 tablespoon crème de cacao

Whipped cream, for decoration (optional)

Grated chocolate, for decoration (optional)

In a small saucepan, combine the espresso, hot chocolate, rum, and crème de cacao. Cook over medium low heat, stirring occasionally, until just heated through. Remove the pan from the heat. Or microwave the mixture in a small microwave-safe container, covered loosely with waxed paper, on medium (50 percent) power for 1 to 2 minutes, or until hot but not boiling.

Pour the hot drink into a large mug. Top with whipped cream and chocolate shavings, if desired. **Serves 1.**

Rum-White Chocolate Espresso: Prepare the Rum-Chocolate Espresso as directed, substituting White Hot Chocolate, (p. 83), for the Hot Chocolate and using only 1 tablespoon of dark rum. Decorate with whipped cream and white chocolate shavings, (p. 55).

Mile-High Ice Cream Pie

A stupendous dessert with an extravagant name, this pie
can be custom-made to suit any ice cream flavor preference.

Graham Cracker Crust:

12 to 14 whole
   graham crackers

¼ teaspoon cinnamon

6 tablespoons unsalted
   butter, melted

½ pint (1 cup) chocolate ice
   cream, slightly softened

¾ pint (1½ cups) orange
   sherbet, slightly softened

1½ pints (3 cups) mint chocolate
   chip ice cream, slightly
   softened

½ cup warm "Hardening" Hot
   Fudge Sauce (p. 87)

Prepare the crust: Preheat the oven to 350°F. In a food processor fitted with the metal blade, process the graham crackers to fine crumbs. Or, using a rolling pin, crush the crackers between 2 pieces of waxed paper to make fine crumbs. You will have about 1½ cups crumbs.

In a small bowl, combine the crumbs, cinnamon, and melted butter; stir until well blended. Using the palm of your hand, press the moistened crumbs into the bottom and up the sides of an ungreased 9-inch pie plate. Bake for 7 to 8 minutes, or until the crust darkens in color. Set on a wire rack to cool completely.

Spread the chocolate ice cream over the bottom of the cooled crust. Freeze for 30 minutes, or until firm. Spread the sherbet over the ice cream and freeze for 30 minutes, or until firm.

Scoop ice cream balls from the mint chocolate chip ice cream and arrange them close together on top of the pie. Return the pie to the freezer until ready to serve.

Just before serving, drizzle the warm fudge sauce over the pie. **Serves 8 to 10.**

"Hardening" Hot Fudge Sauce

This glossy, fudgy sauce magically turns chewy and candylike upon contact with cold ice cream. If you prefer it more runny, boil the sauce uncovered for 3 minutes rather than 5.

2 ounces unsweetened
   chocolate, coarsely chopped
2 tablespoons unsalted butter
½ cup water

1 cup plus 2 tablespoons sugar
2 tablespoons light corn syrup
2 teaspoons pure vanilla extract

In a heavy medium-size saucepan, combine the chocolate, butter, and water. Cook over medium-low heat, stirring constantly, until the chocolate is melted and smooth. Stir in the sugar and corn syrup. Cook over medium heat, stirring frequently, until the sauce comes to a full boil. Reduce the heat to low, cover, and cook for 2 minutes to dissolve any sugar crystals on the side of the pan. Do not stir.

Uncover the saucepan and boil over low heat, without stirring, for 5 minutes.

Remove the pan from the heat and let cool for 5 minutes. Stir in the vanilla. Use immediately. The sauce will thicken as it cools. **Makes about 1¼ cups.**

NOTE: Store the sauce in the refrigerator in an airtight container for up to 3 weeks. Reheat it in the top of a double boiler set over barely simmering (not boiling) water, or in a microwave-safe container, loosely covered, on low (30 percent) power for 1 to 2 minutes, stirring once.

Coffee Hot Fudge Sundae

*Stirring a little rum or coffee-flavored liqueur into the warm fudge sauce
makes this a very grown-up dessert, particularly since the sauce is teamed with
premium coffee ice cream. For more traditional hot fudge sundaes, omit the spirits,
use vanilla ice cream, and top with whipped cream and chopped nuts.*

¾ cup warm "Hardening" Hot
    Fudge Sauce (p. 87)

1 tablespoon dark rum
    or coffee-flavored liqueur
    (Kahlúa)

1½ pints (3 cups) coffee ice
    cream

Chopped walnuts, for
    decoration (optional)

Prepare the "Hardening" Hot Fudge Sauce according to the recipe. Stir the rum into the warm sauce. Spoon about 1 tablespoon of the sauce into each of 4 sundae dishes or stemmed glasses. Top with large scoops of the coffee ice cream and spoon more warm sauce over the top. Decorate with chopped walnuts, if desired. **Serves 4.**

Thoroughly Modern Banana Split

This updated version of a banana split may be more restrained than the 1950s soda fountain giant, but it remains a glorious splurge. Use premium vanilla ice cream and the reddest, sweetest raspberries you can find. If raspberries are not in season, substitute strawberries.

6 tablespoons warm
"Hardening" Hot Fudge
Sauce (p. 87)

1 large ripe banana

2 generous scoops vanilla
ice cream

6 heaping tablespoons (about
4 ounces) fresh raspberries

Whipped cream, for decoration

1/4 cup chopped toasted walnuts,
for decoration

Prepare the "Hardening" Hot Fudge Sauce according to the recipe. Peel the banana and cut it half. Slice each half lengthwise into 4. Arrange 4 slices of banana around the sides of each of 2 sundae dishes or stemmed glasses, with the pointed ends up.

Spoon 1 scoop of ice cream into the center of each dish and spoon the hot fudge sauce over and around the ice cream. Reserve 2 of the best-looking, largest raspberries for decoration and sprinkle the remaining raspberries evenly over the ice cream. Top with whipped cream. Scatter the nuts over the whipped cream and decorate with the reserved raspberries. **Serves 2.**

Alkalized cocoa powder: Also called Dutch-processed. Cocoa powder that has been processed with an alkali to neutralize the natural acidity of chocolate is labeled "alkalized" or "treated with an alkali." It looks darker than nonalkalized cocoa, but its flavor is milder.

Baking chocolate: Although you can bake with all types of chocolate, when a recipe calls for baking chocolate, it is referring to unsweetened or bitter chocolate.

Bittersweet chocolate: Also called dark chocolate. Bittersweet chocolate is made from chocolate liquor that is sweetened with sugar and blended with cocoa butter, lecithin (an emulsifier), and flavorings such as vanilla or vanillin. It is the ratio of chocolate liquor to the other ingredients that puts the chocolate in this category: Bittersweet chocolate must be at least 35 percent chocolate liquor. In the recipes in this book, bittersweet chocolate may be used interchangeably with semisweet, according to your personal taste. In general, European dark chocolates are labeled "bittersweet," while American dark chocolates are labeled "semisweet."

Cacao: The cacao tree, grown in South and Central America, Africa, Southeast Asia, and the West Indies, is cultivated for its seed pods (cocoa beans), which are used to produce chocolate.

Chocolate bloom: Improperly stored chocolate may develop powdery-looking white blotches, or its surface may turn grainy and rough. Both conditions are referred to as bloom. The first is fat bloom, caused by a warm environment; the second is sugar bloom, caused by a damp environment. Neither condition makes the chocolate unfit for eating or cooking. When the chocolate is melted, the bloom disappears.

Chocolate liquor: During processing, the nibs, or meat, of the cocoa bean are heated and ground into a thick paste. This is pure chocolate containing on average a little more than 50 percent cocoa butter. From this product come all other forms of chocolate (semisweet, milk, etc.). When allowed to harden, it becomes unsweetened chocolate.

Cocoa butter: Cocoa beans contain a fat called cocoa butter. It is added to some chocolate in varying amounts during further processing. Cocoa butter, which is solid fat, allows chocolate to break with a clean snap, to shine, and to melt smoothly.

Cocoa powder: After most of the cocoa butter is removed from chocolate liquor, the liquor can be pressed and ground into cocoa powder. Cocoa powder is therefore not fat-free: It is still 22 percent cocoa butter. Cocoa powder is either natural (nonalkalized) or alkalized.

Conching: In the chocolate-making process, after the cocoa beans are fermented, roasted, and refined, the chocolate is conched. During refining, the chocolate is rolled between heavy rollers, and ingredients such as sugar and milk solids are added. During conching, the warm refined chocolate is kneaded and mellowed for 12 to 72 hours. The length of conching affects the texture of the finished chocolate.

Confectionery coating: Also called summer coatings and compound coatings, confectionery coatings are not considered chocolate. These candy-making ingredients are made from cocoa powder and/or dried milk, sugar, and a solid vegetable fat. White chocolate is also referred to as confectionery coating by U.S. manufacturers. If you want white chocolate, read the label carefully to make sure the product contains cocoa butter, not vegetable fat.

Couverture chocolate: This term applies to high-quality dark chocolate with a high percentage of cocoa butter. Couverture is the chocolate used by professionals and home cooks alike for enrobing (coating), hand-dipping, and molding. It melts smoothly and forms a thin shell with a lovely shine and snap.

Dark chocolate: This term refers to sweetened chocolate liquor that contains no milk solids, such as bittersweet and semisweet chocolate.

Dutch-processed cocoa: This is another term for alkalized cocoa.

Ganache: When warm, melted chocolate is combined with cream, it forms a mixture called ganache. Depending on its temperature and consistency, ganache can be formed into truffles or used as a frosting, filling, or sauce.

Milk chocolate: Milk solids, cocoa butter, and flavorings such as vanilla and vanillin are added to sweetened chocolate liquor to make milk chocolate. Because the proteins in the solids make it sensitive to heat, milk chocolate can not be substituted for dark chocolate in a recipe.

Nonalkalized cocoa powder: Also called natural cocoa powder, nonalkalized cocoa powder has not been treated with an alkali and so is more acidic than alkalized cocoa. It has a lighter color but a bolder chocolate flavor. Be sure to use the type of cocoa specified in the recipe.

Seizing: Seizing occurs when a small amount of water or moisture in melted chocolate causes it to lump and harden. To prevent seizing, see Care and Handling of Chocolate, page 94.

Semisweet chocolate: Similar in composition to bittersweet chocolate, semisweet chocolate is also at least 35 percent chocolate liquor. Because they contain the same amount of chocolate liquor, the two can be used interchangeably.

Sweet chocolate: First produced by a Mr. German, this chocolate is a blend of 15 percent chocolate liquor and cocoa butter, sugar, milk solids, and flavorings. Sweet chocolate should not be substituted for dark chocolate, because it contains less chocolate liquor.

Temper: Chocolate is in temper when it leaves the manufacturer, which means the cocoa butter crystals are stable. When chocolate is melted it goes out of temper. It also loses its temper when it is improperly stored (see Care and Handling of Chocolate). The process of tempering stabilizes the cocoa butter crystals by melting and cooling the chocolate to a certain temperature. Tempering is necessary for some candy making, and for enrobing and molding chocolate. It is not necessary for any recipe in this book.

Unsweetened chocolate: This is sometimes called plain, bitter, or baking chocolate. It is nothing more than refined chocolate (chocolate liquor) with no added sugar.

White chocolate: White chocolate is made from sugar, cocoa butter, milk solids, lecithin, and flavorings. The U.S. Standards of Identity doesn't recognize this product as chocolate, because it contains no chocolate liquor. In Europe, it is called white chocolate. Here manufacturers often refer to it as confectionery coating or summer coating. However, some of these so-named products contain vegetable fat instead of cocoa butter and should not be used in recipes calling for white chocolate. Read all labels carefully.

CARE AND HANDLING OF CHOCOLATE

STORING: All solid chocolate should be stored at cool room temperature (65°F and 50 percent relative humidity are ideal), wrapped in foil, then in plastic. Dark chocolate will keep for a decade if stored properly. White and milk chocolate keep for eight months and one year, respectively. Do not refrigerate or freeze chocolate.

MELTING: Chocolate can be melted using a double boiler or a microwave oven. Both methods require attention, but, if carefully monitored, are not difficult.

Melting chocolate in a double boiler set over water can result in stiffening, or seizing. This occurs when the tiniest droplet of moisture (from steam or a splash) gets into the melted chocolate. When this happens, what was a smooth, velvety pool of chocolate turns to a nasty, stiff, lumpy mess. Heating, stirring, or beating will not return the chocolate to its liquid state. To prevent seizing, be sure the water in the bottom of the double boiler is at least ½ inch below the bottom of the top pan and that it *never* comes to a boil. Even a good simmer produces steam and potential disaster. Ideally, the water used to melt chocolate should be between 120° and 140°F. Seizing is not a problem when chocolate is melted with cream or other ingredients.

Chocolate melted in the microwave oven can scorch if left too long. It's best to melt it at medium (50 percent) power and check it frequently after the first minute. Take the chocolate out of the microwave when it turns shiny and soft and then stir it until smooth and melted; it will not melt to a liquid pool inside the microwave.

WEIGHTS

Ounces and Pounds	Metrics
¼ ounce	7 grams
⅓ ounce	10 grams
½ ounce	14 grams
1 ounce	28 grams
1½ ounces	42 grams
1¾ ounces	50 grams
2 ounces	57 grams
3 ounces	85 grams
3½ ounces	100 grams
4 ounces (¼ pound)	114 grams
6 ounces	170 grams
8 ounces (½ pound)	227 grams
9 ounces	250 grams
16 ounces (1 pound)	464 grams

LIQUID MEASURES

tsp.: teaspoon
Tbs.: tablespoon

Spoons and Cups	Metric Equivalents
¼ tsp.	1.23 milliliters
½ tsp.	2.5 milliliters
¾ tsp.	3.7 milliliters
1 tsp.	5 milliliters
1 dessertspoon	10 milliliters
1 Tbs. (3 tsp.)	15 milliliters
2 Tbs. (1 ounce)	30 milliliters
¼ cup	60 milliliters
⅓ cup	80 milliliters
½ cup	120 milliliters
⅔ cup	160 milliliters
¾ cup	180 milliliters
1 cup (8 ounces)	240 milliliters
2 cups (1 pint)	480 milliliters
3 cups	720 milliliters
4 cups (1 quart)	1 litre
4 quarts (1 gallon)	3¾ litres

TEMPERATURES

°F (Fahrenheit)	°C (Centigrade or Celsius)
32 (water freezes)	0
200	95
212 (water boils)	100
250	120
275	135
300 (slow oven)	150
325	160
350 (moderate oven)	175
375	190
400 (hot oven)	205
425	220
450 (very hot oven)	232
475	245
500 (extremely hot oven)	260

LENGTH

U.S. Measurements	Metric Equivalents
⅛ inch	3mm
¼ inch	6mm
⅜ inch	1 cm
½ inch	1.2 cm
¾ inch	2 cm
1 inch	2.5 cm
1¼ inches	3.1 cm
1½ inches	3.7 cm
2 inches	5 cm
3 inches	7.5 cm
4 inches	10 cm
5 inches	12.5 cm

APPROXIMATE EQUIVALENTS

1 kilo is slightly more than 2 pounds
1 litre is slightly more than 1 quart
1 meter is slightly over 3 feet
1 centimeter is approximately ⅜ inch

TRADE

MARK

CHOCOLATE

BROWNIE
BAND

THE WORD "BROWNIES" COPYRIGHTED NOVEMBER 22, 1887

12

FOR **1** CENT